Reading fluency

To support children in developing fluency in their reading, you can give them plenty of opportunities to revisit the books. These include:
- rereading independently
- rereading with a partner
- rereading at home
- hearing the book read to them as they follow the printed text.

Rereading and rehearing helps children develop automatic word recognition and gives them models of fluent, expressive reading.

Comprehension strategies

Title	Comprehension strategy taught through these Teaching Notes				
	Prediction	Questioning	Clarifying	Summarising	Imagining
Diamonds	✓	✓	✓	✓	✓
Using a Computer		✓	✓	✓	✓
Robots	✓	✓	✓	✓	✓
Comic Illustrators	✓	✓	✓	✓	✓
Training Like an Athlete	✓	✓	✓	✓	✓
Environmental Disasters	✓	✓	✓	✓	✓

Vocabulary and phonic opportunities

The chart shows the main words used in each book. The decodable words listed should be decidable for most children at this Stage. The tricky words are common but do not conform to the phonic rules taught up to this point – children will need support to learn and recognise them. If children struggle with one of these words you can model how to read it.

Diamonds	High frequency decodable words	deep, mine, miners, rock, hard, cut, polished, used, large, smaller, carat
	High frequency tricky words	diamonds, weigh, colour, jewellery
Using a Computer	High frequency decodable words	computer, smaller, better, first, change, letter, text, poster, drawing, photograph, Internet, e-mail, school, printer
	High frequency tricky words	electricity, colour, picture(s)
Robots	High frequency decodable words	robot, job(s), arm(s), program, box, bulb, holder, control
	High frequency tricky words	human, move, movements, instructions, machine
Comic Illustrators	High frequency decodable words	children, comic, strip, drew, funny, Roman, drawing, story
	High frequency tricky words	illustrator, character, stories, newspaper, famous, people, idea, picture(s)
Training Like an Athlete	High frequency decodable words	athlete, good, ball, very, playing, player(s), won, hot, tennis, football, sport, they, training, golf, every, makes
	High frequency tricky words	competitive
Environmental Disasters	High frequency decodable words	disasters, oil, spilled, toxic, gas, nuclear, smog, kill, animals, water, fish, bird(s), firefighters
	High frequency tricky words	pollution, spread(s), accident, dangerous, radioactive

Teaching Notes

Contents

Introduction

Fireflies is an exciting non-fiction series within *Oxford Reading Tree*. These books are specially designed to be used alongside the Stage 9 stories. They provide practice of reading skills in a non-fiction context whilst using the same simple, repetitive sentence structures as the *Oxford Reading Tree* stories. They also contain a selection of decodable and tricky words. Each stage builds on the reading skills and vocabulary from previous stages. Each book offers scope for developing children's word recognition and language comprehension skills in a highly motivating way, whilst also providing strong cross-curricular links.

To help children approach each new book in this stage with confidence, you should prepare the children for reading by talking about the book and asking questions. You can use these Teaching Notes and the additional notes in the inside front and back covers of the pupil books to help you. The notes within the pupil books can also be used by parents or teaching assistants.

Using the books

This booklet provides suggestions for using the books for guided, group and independent activities. The reading activities include ideas for developing children's *word recognition* **W** and *language comprehension* **C** skills. Within word recognition, there are ideas for helping children practise their phonic skills and knowledge, as well as helping them tackle words which are not easy to decode phonically. The language comprehension ideas include suggestions for teaching the skills of prediction, questioning, clarifying, summarising and imagining, in order to help children understand the texts. Suggestions are also provided for speaking and listening and writing activities, as well as for introducing linked electronic material and cross-curricular links.

Curriculum coverage chart

	Speaking and listening activities	Reading	Writing
Diamonds			
PNS Literacy Framework (Y2)	1.3	Ⓦ 5.3 Ⓒ 7.1, 7.2, 7.4	9.5, 11.2
National Curriculum	Working within Level 2		
Scotland (5–14) (P3)	Level A/B		
N. Ireland (P3/Y3)	1, 3, 9, 11	1, 2, 4, 6, 8, 10	1, 3, 4, 6, 7, 8, 10, 11, 12
Wales (Key Stage 1)	Range: 1, 2 Skills: 1, 2, 3	Range: 1, 2, 3 Skills: 1, 2, 4	Range: 1, 2, 3, 4, 5, 7 Skills: 1, 4, 5, 6, 7, 8, 9
	Speaking and listening activities	**Reading**	**Writing**
Using a Computer			
PNS Literacy Framework (Y2)	2.1	Ⓦ 5.5 Ⓒ 7.1, 7.2, 7.3	9.5
National Curriculum	Working within Level 2		
Scotland (5–14) (P3)	Level A/B		
N. Ireland (P3/Y3)	1, 3, 5, 6, 11, 13	1, 3, 4, 6, 7, 8, 9, 11	1, 3, 4, 5, 6, 8, 10, 11, 12, 13
Wales (Key Stage 1)	Range: 1, 2, 3 Skills: 1, 3, 4, 5, 6	Range: 1, 2, 3, 4 Skills: 1, 2, 4	Range: 1, 2, 3, 4, 5, 7 Skills: 1, 2, 4, 5, 6, 7, 8

Key

Ⓒ = Language comprehension   Y = Year

Ⓦ = Word recognition   P = Primary

In the designations such as 5.2, the first number represents the strand and the second number the bullet point.

Curriculum coverage chart

	Speaking and listening activities	Reading	Writing
Robots			
PNS Literacy Framework (Y2)	1.1, 4.1	**W** 5.3 **C** 7.1, 7.2, 7.3, 7.4	9.4
National Curriculum	Working within Level 2		
Scotland (5–14) (P3)	Level A/B		
N. Ireland (P3/Y3)	1, 5, 10, 11	1, 3, 4, 5, 6, 8, 9, 10, 11, 12, 14, 15, 16, 17	1, 2, 3, 4, 5, 6, 7, 8, 10, 11, 13
Wales (Key Stage 1)	Range: 1, 2, 3, 5 Skills: 1, 2, 3, 5	Range: 1, 2, 3, 4 Skills: 1, 2, 4	Range: 1, 2, 3, 4, 5, 7 Skills: 1, 4, 5, 7, 8
	Speaking and listening activities	**Reading**	**Writing**
Comic Illustrators			
PNS Literacy Framework (Y2)	1.1	**W** 5.3 **C** 7.1, 7.4, 8.2	10.1, 10.2
National Curriculum	Working within Level 2		
Scotland (5–14) (P3)	Level A/B		
N. Ireland (P3/Y3)	1, 2, 3, 6, 7, 10, 11, 12, 13	1, 3, 4, 6, 8, 9, 10, 11, 12, 14, 15, 16, 17	1, 2, 3, 5, 6, 7, 8, 10, 11, 12, 13
Wales (Key Stage 1)	Range: 1, 2, 5 Skills: 1, 2, 3	Range: 1, 2, 3, 4 Skills: 1, 2, 4	Range: 1, 2, 3, 4, 5, 7 Skills: 1, 2, 4, 5, 6, 7, 8, 9

Curriculum coverage chart

	Speaking and listening activities	Reading	Writing
Training Like an Athlete			
PNS Literacy Framework (Y2)	2.1, 4.1	W 6.1 C 7.1, 7.3, 8.3	9.5
National Curriculum	Working within Level 2		
Scotland (5–14) (P3)	Level A/B		
N. Ireland (P3/Y3)	1, 6, 8, 9, 10, 11, 12	1, 3, 4, 5, 6, 7, 8, 9, 10, 11, 12, 14, 15, 16, 17	1, 2, 3, 4, 5, 6, 7, 10, 11
Wales (Key Stage 1)	Range: 1, 2, 3, 5 Skills: 1, 2, 3, 4, 5, 6	Range: 1, 2, 3, 4 Skills: 1, 2, 4	Range: 1, 2, 3, 7 Skills: 1, 4, 5, 8
	Speaking and listening activities	**Reading**	**Writing**
Environmental Disasters			
PNS Literacy Framework (Y2)	2.1, 4.1	W 5.4, 6.2 C 7.1, 7.4, 8.2	9.5, 11.1
National Curriculum	Working towards Level 3		
Scotland (5–14) (P3)	Level A/B		
N. Ireland (P3/Y3)	1, 3, 6, 7, 8, 9, 10, 11, 12	1, 3, 4, 5, 6, 8, 10, 11, 12, 14, 15, 16, 17	1, 2, 3, 4, 5, 6, 7, 8, 10, 11, 12
Wales (Key Stage 1)	Range: 1, 2, 3, 5, 6 Skills: 1, 2, 3, 4, 5, 6	Range: 1, 2, 3, 4 Skills: 1, 2, 4	Range: 1, 2, 3, 7 Skills: 1, 5, 6, 7, 8, 9

Diamonds

> **C** = Language comprehension   *R, AF* = QCA reading assessment focus
>
> **W** = Word recognition   *W, AF* = QCA writing assessment focus

Group or guided reading

Introducing the book

C *(Clarifying)* Look at the cover and read the title together. Ask: *Have you ever seen a diamond? What was it like? Did it shine?*

C *(Prediction)* Ask: *What do you think this book is going to tell us about diamonds?*

Strategy check

Remind the children of the strategies they can use to work out a word: sound it out; break it up into syllables; look for two words within the whole word.

Independent reading

● Ask children to read the book aloud. Praise and encourage them while they read, and prompt as necessary.

C *(Summarising)* Ask them to make note of the three countries mentioned where diamonds are found.

W Help children with the tricky words 'valuable', 'precious', 'sapphire', 'facets' and 'sceptre'.

Assessment Check that children:

● *(R, AF1)* read high frequency words with confidence

● *(R, AF1)* use a variety of strategies to work out new words

● *(R, AF2)* use comprehension skills to retrieve information.

Returning to the text

C *(Summarising)* Ask: *Was the information in the book as you predicted?* Discuss children's predictions and how close they were to the content of the book. Were there things they expected which weren't in the book?

(C) *(Clarifying)* Ask children to tell you the names of the countries mentioned in the book. Look at the world map on pages 8 and 9 and pinpoint South Africa, Namibia and India. Ask: *What type of diamond mine is here, big or small? Check with the key.*

(W) On page 12 ask the children to find as many words as they can with the root word 'weigh'. ('weight', 'weighed', 'weights', 'weighing') Say: *Tell me the suffixes.*

Group and independent reading activities

Objective Draw together ideas and information from across a whole text, using simple signposts in the text (7.1).

You will need postcards with one of the following questions on each:
Why is the way a diamond important?
What is the weight of a diamond measured in?
What colour can diamonds be?
Find two uses for diamonds.
Where are diamonds found?

(C) *(Clarifying)* Group the children into pairs and give them a question card.

● Pairs find the answer to the question, by using the Contents or Index, then write it down.

● They swap question cards with another group and repeat.

● When all groups have answered all the questions, record answers on the board and discuss the best way of finding information in a book.

Assessment *(R, AF2)* Do children use the Contents and Index to find the answers?

(W) Know how to tackle unfamiliar words that are not completely decodable (5.3).

● Look at the 'tricky' words listed in the 'independent reading' section of these notes. Ask children to tell you ways that they might work out the words. Did they suggest breaking the words up into syllables? Did they split the words up into phonemes?

Assessment *(R, AF1)* Do children pronounce 'facets' correctly?

Objective Use syntax and context to build their store of vocabulary when reading for meaning (7.4).

- **C** *(Clarifying)* Encourage children to tell you some new words that they found in the text and write them on the board, e.g. 'valuable' (page 3), 'colourless' (page 10), 'precious' (page 11), 'flaws' (page 17).

- Ask them to tell you the meaning of the words from their context.

- Encourage them to check the meaning by looking at the glossary or a dictionary.

Assessment *(R, AF1)* Do children find out the meaning of new words by using context?

Objective Give some reasons why things happen (7.2).

- **C** *(Imagining, Questioning)* Discuss the introduction on page 3.

- Ask: *Why are diamonds no longer found in rivers and streams?*

- Explain that the text doesn't actually say why but can anyone suggest a reason.

- Discuss children's suggestions and record on the board.

- Encourage children to try and find out with your help the reason why diamonds cannot be found in streams.

Assessment *(R, AF3)* Do children make reasoned suggestions using knowledge gleaned from the rest of the text?

E-links

E-Fireflies

This book is available electronically, on *e-Fireflies Stages 7–10* CD-ROM. You can read the text as a 'Talking Book' on a whiteboard with the whole class, or on a computer with a group of children. Use the tools to annotate the text with the children. The children can then use 'Make a Book' to select their own choice of content and make their own books. Use the Teacher Settings screen to select how you want any part of the CD-ROM to be used, and the Progress Report Chart to track the progress of individual children.

Speaking and listening activities

Objective Explain ideas and processes using imaginative and adventurous vocabulary and non-verbal gestures to support communication (1.3).

● Ask the children to work in pairs to create a spider diagram of what they have learned about diamonds from the book.

● They then use the spider diagram to prepare a short talk to give to the rest of the group or class. They could choose one aspect of what they have learned if they prefer, e.g. the crown jewels.

● Encourage the children to practise their talk and to make sure what they say is clear and interesting to the listener.

Cross-curricular links: National Curriculum Key Stage 1

Geography
Pupils should be taught to:

● Use globes, maps and plans at a range of scales

Writing activities

Objectives Select from different presentational features to suit particular writing purposes on paper and on screen (9.5).
Compose sentences using tense consistently (present and past) (11.2).

● Ask the children to pretend to be Kind Edward VII. He has just received the Star of Africa and he wants to write a thank you letter to Mr Cullinan in South Africa.

● Discuss what the king might say in his letter. For example, he might say: how beautiful it is; how very pleased he is to have it; what he is going to do with it and where it is going to be kept.

● Talk about what tense the letter will be written in (present).

● Remind the children that because it is from the king the language is going to be very formal and polite.

Assessment *(W, AF6)* Do children use the correct tense throughout?

Using a Computer

C = Language comprehension   *R, AF* = QCA reading assessment focus

W = Word recognition   *W, AF* = QCA writing assessment focus

Group or guided reading

Introducing the book

C *(Clarifying)* Look at the cover and read the title together. Ask: *Do you enjoy using a computer? What do you use the computer for?*

C *(Imagining)* Say: *Tell me some other things you know computers are used for. Do you think computers are useful things? Can you imagine what it was like before computers were invented?*

Strategy check

Remind the children of the ways of finding information in a non-fiction book: the contents and index.

Independent reading

● Ask children to read the book aloud. Praise and encourage them while they read, and prompt as necessary.

C *(Summarising)* Ask children to make a note of the dates mentioned in the book.

W Remind the children that the words in bold are words that can be found in the glossary at the back of the book. Ask: *What is a glossary?*

W Ask the children to note down any words they come across that have anything to do with computers.

Assessment Check that children:

● *(R, AF1)* read high frequency words with confidence

● *(R, AF1)* use a variety of strategies to work out new words

● *(R, AF2)* use comprehension skills to retrieve information.

Returning to the text

C *(Summarising)* Ask the children to tell you briefly about the book and one interesting fact about computers they didn't know before reading the book.

W Ask the children to tell you the words they found whilst reading that have something to do with computers. Record these on the board and discuss the methods they used to decode the words, e.g. 'Internet' (breaking up into syllables), 'website' (splitting the word into two words), 'scanner' (sounding out the phonemes 's-c-a-nn-e-r').

C *(Questioning)* On page 7 ask the children to tell you which is the quickest way to make a poster – by computer or by hand? Ask: *Do they think this is always the case?*

Group and independent reading activities

Objective Explain organisational features of texts, including diagrams (7.3).

C *(Clarifying, Summarising)* Ask children to tell you the dates they noted down in the 'independent reading' section of these notes.

- Write them on the board and discuss in which order the dates should appear: 1642, 1931, 1945, 1975.
- Show the children how to draw a timeline using the dates. Discuss the position of the numbers on the line.
- Ask children to tell you what event happened on each date.
- Encourage them to draw their own history of computers timeline, filling in the dates, what happened and drawing a picture.
- Some children may want to put in the present year's date and talk about the most up-to-date technology information, e.g. handheld computers.
- Display the timelines.

Assessment *(R, AF2)* Do children retrieve the correct information from the book?

W Read high and medium frequency words independently and automatically (5.5).

You will need a set of cards with the following words: 'paste', 'cut', 'copy', 'save', 'open', 'undo', 'bold', 'italic', 'underline', 'new' and a set of cards with the matching icons for each word.

(W) In small groups play Pelmanism with the cards.

- Turn the cards face down.
- Children take it in turns to turn up the cards to see if they can match up the words with the icons.
- Keep going until all the cards have a pair.

Assessment *(R, AF1)* Do children read the words without hesitation?

Objective Give some reasons why things happen (7.2).

(C) *(Clarifying, Questioning, Imagining)* Turn to page 5 and talk about why computers changed from being really large to the small PCs, laptops and handheld computers we have today.

- Ask: *Why was it important to make computers smaller?* (to fit on a desk or in a bag, to be cheaper to run, to be available for most people, etc.)
- Ask: *How do you think computers are going to change in the next few years? What will come next? What would you like to be able to use a computer for when you are grown up?*

Assessment *(R, AF3)* Can the children find the information in the text to support their answers?

Objectives Draw together ideas and information from across a whole text, using simple signposts in the text (7.1).
Explain organisational features of texts, including alphabetical order (7.3).

(C) *(Summarising)* Ask the children to find the information about one of the items listed in the Index, e.g. 'website'.

- Remind them to tell you on what page the information can be found.
- Repeat for other words.
- Ask them to read pages 3–5 and pick out words they think could be added to the Index.

- Note the words on the board and, with the children's help, place them in alphabetical order.

Assessment *(R, AF2)* Do children place 'television' before 'traffic lights'?

Speaking and listening activities

Objective Listen to others in class, ask relevant questions and follow instructions (2.1).

- Children work in pairs at a computer. Using pages 9–10 for reference, the children take turns to give each other instructions on how to change the font style.
- Repeat with how to change the layout or adding colour (pages 11 and 12).
- Talk about how to make the instructions as clear and precise as possible.

Cross-curricular links: National Curriculum Key Stage 1

ICT
Pupils should be taught:

- How to share their ideas by presenting information in a variety of terms [for example text, images, tables, sounds]

Writing activities

Objective Select from different presentational features to suit particular writing purposes on paper and on screen (9.5).

- Talk about any upcoming school events.
- Say that the children are going to design a poster advertising the event.
- In pairs, children should plan and design an eye-catching poster detailing all the information about the event.
- They can refer to the book if they need to.
- Encourage them to use artwork on their poster. What do they use and how do they go about getting it on to their poster?

Assessment *(W, AF2)* Do the children use different font styles and sizes?

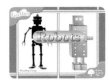

Robots

> **C** = Language comprehension   *R, AF* = QCA reading assessment focus
>
> **W** = Word recognition   *W, AF* = QCA writing assessment focus

Group or guided reading

Introducing the book

C *(Clarifying)* Look at the cover and read the title together. Ask: *What do you know about robots?*

C *(Prediction)* Ask: *What do you think the book will tell us about robots?*

Strategy check

Remind the children of the different strategies they can use to work out new words, e.g. break up into syllables, sound out the phonemes, use context by reading to the end of the sentence.

Independent reading

● Ask children to read the book aloud. Praise and encourage them while they read, and prompt as necessary.

C *(Summarising)* Ask them to take note of the different ways that robots are used.

W Point out the word 'wriggle' on page 8. Ask: *What other words do you know that begin with 'wr'?* ('wrong', 'write', 'wrist'.)

Assessment Check that children:

● *(R, AF1)* read high frequency words with confidence

● *(R, AF1)* use a variety of strategies to work out new words

● *(R, AF2)* use comprehension skills to retrieve information.

Returning to the text

C *(Summarising, Questioning)* Say: *Tell me some of the ways robots are used. Which use do you find the most interesting and why?*

W On page 3 ask the children why '*Star Wars*' is written in italics.

(c) *(Clarifying, Questioning)* Ask: *Why do sheep have to be sheared? What happens to the sheep's wool?*

(w) Turn to page 7. Discuss pronouncing the word 'breathe'. Ask: *What happens when the 'e' is taken off?*

(c) *(Clarifying)* On page 8 ask: *What are sensors? Some animals have sensors, what sort of animals?* (Antennae on insects.)

Group and independent reading activities

Objective Explain organisational features of texts, including diagrams (7.3).

(c) *(Questioning)* Look at pages 14 to 17. Discuss the way the information is laid out and the use of the diagrams.

● Ask: *Do you think this is a good way of showing the reader how to do something? How do the diagrams help? How is the layout of these pages different to the layout of the text on pages 8 and 9?*

● Point out how the numbers next to each diagram relate to the numbers in the written instructions. Ask: *Is this helpful?*

Assessment *(R, AF4)* Can the children tell you the differences between the layouts?

Objectives Know how to tackle unfamiliar words that are not completely decodable (5.3).
Use syntax and context to build their store of vocabulary when reading for meaning (7.4).

You will need cards with the following words on them: 'automatically', 'situations', 'medicine', 'precise', 'detect'.

(w) Hold up the cards and discuss the number of syllables in the words.

● List the words under headings, e.g. '6 syllables', '4 syllables', etc.

● Discuss other ways that the children worked out the words.

● Talk about the meaning of each of the words. Did the children look at the context to work out its meaning?

● Children should check meaning using a dictionary.

Assessment *(R, AF1)* Do children accurately decode the words?

Objective Give some reasons why things happen (7.2).

(C) *(Clarifying, Imagining, Questioning)* Discuss why humans invented robots.

● Read through the first half of the book listing the advantages robots have over humans, e.g. they do not breathe so they can go to places like the moon; they can make small, precise movements, etc.

● Ask: *What are the disadvantages of robots?*

Assessment *(R, AF3)* Can the children retrieve information from the text?

Objective Draw together ideas and information from across a whole text, using simple signposts in the text (7.1).

You will need some question cards with the following questions on:
Name a film that robots appear in.
What does Shear Magic do?
What does Robosaurus do to cars?
How many light bulbs are needed to make the model robot?
What can robots do to bombs?

(C) *(Clarifying)* Encourage the children to use the Index and Contents page in the book to find the answers to the questions.

Assessment *(R, AF3)* Do children use the Index or Contents to find the answers?

E-links

Fireflies Plus

If you are an Espresso user, you can access videos, quizzes and activities linked to this title to enrich your children's reading. Children can also write, post and compare reviews of the book. Full supporting Teaching Notes for this content are available on the site in PDF format. Within the Espresso site, follow the route **<Channel guide → English 1 → Oxford Reading Tree Fireflies Plus logo>**. *Espresso Primary* is an extensive library of cross-curricular, video-rich broadband teaching resources and learning activities that motivates children and supports teachers.

Speaking and listening activities

Objectives Speak with clarity and use appropriate intonation (1.1).
Adopt appropriate roles in small or large groups (4.1).

- Ask the children to imagine they have a 'Meldog'. In pairs, ask them to prepare some instructions for Meldog to help them to tidy their bedroom, e.g. dusting, sweeping the floor, picking things up off the floor, cleaning the windows, making the bed, etc.

- One child pretends to be Meldog and the other gives clear and polite instructions to Meldog to carry out the tasks.

- Ask for feedback on how easy/difficult it was to give the instructions.

Cross-curricular links

ICT
Pupils should be taught:

- How to plan and give instructions to make things happen

Writing activities

Objective Make adventurous word and language choices appropriate to the style and purpose of the text (9.4).

- Turn to page 9 and discuss the information about Robosaurus.

- Say to the children that they are newspaper reporters and they are going to write a report on what happened when they went to see a Robosaurus show. Ask them to imagine they are sitting in the red seats in the photograph.

- Talk about the sort of things people will want to know about the Robosaurus: what it looks like; what it does and how it does it; is it exciting to see? What are the best bits?

- Encourage children to use imaginative language in their descriptions.

Assessment *(W, AF7)* Do children make sensible and effective word choices?

Comic Illustrators

C = Language comprehension   **R, AF** = QCA reading assessment focus

W = Word recognition   **W, AF** = QCA writing assessment focus

Group or guided reading

Introducing the book

C *(Clarifying)* Look at the cover and read the title together. Ask: *Why is the heading in a speech bubble? What does an illustrator do?*

C *(Prediction)* Ask: *Do you have a favourite comic you like reading? Do you have a favourite comic character? Do you ever like to draw cartoons? Which cartoons would you like to read about?*

Strategy check

Remind the children of the ways of finding information in a non-fiction book: by looking in the Contents and Index.

Independent reading

- Ask children to read the book aloud. Praise and encourage them while they read, and prompt as necessary.

C *(Summarising)* Ask children to make a note of the fictional characters and the real people described in the book.

W Point out to the children that there is no glossary in this book, but some of the words appear in colour in the text and there is a definition in a 'zig-zag' bubble on the same page.

W Help children with the tricky words 'sweater', 'knights', 'magicians', 'Schulz', 'Schroeder', 'Goscinny', 'talent'.

Assessment Check that children:

- *(R, AF1)* read high frequency words with confidence
- *(R, AF1)* use a variety of strategies to work out new words
- *(R, AF2)* use comprehension skills to retrieve information.

Returning to the text

C *(Summarising)* Ask the children to tell you briefly about one of the fictional characters and one of the real life characters.

W On the board write the headings 'ea' (long sound) and 'ee' (short sound). Ask the children to find words for each heading. They should find for 'ea': 'bear', 'wear', 'sweater', 'their', 'fairy'. For 'ee' they should find: 'appeal', 'Peanuts', 'reason', 'real', 'feelings', 'seaside', 'teacher', 'team', 'Greece', 'agreed', 'speech'.

W Turn to pages 8 and 10 and discuss the sound that 'Sch' makes in 'Schulz' and 'Schroeder'. Ask: *Do you know another word that begins 'sch' but is said in a different way?* (school)

C *(Clarifying)* Ask the children to show you a caption. Ask: *What is it in the form of? Why has the book designer decided to do this?* Get the children to think of another style the captions could have been in.

Group and independent reading activities

Objective Draw together ideas and information from across a whole text, using simple signposts in the text (7.1).

C *(Clarifying, Summarising, Questioning)* Arrange the children into three groups to write questions for a quiz. One group is to work on Rupert Bear, the second on Peanuts and the third on Asterix.

● Remind the children of the different question words they could use: who, where, what, when, how.

● Ask the children to prepare six questions and to write them out on separate pieces of card with the answers on the back.

● The children should then ask each other their questions, checking with the book where necessary.

Assessment *(R, AF2)* Do the children use the Contents and Index to find the answers to the questions?

W Know how to tackle unfamiliar words that are not completely decodable (5.3).

● Look at the 'tricky' words listed in the 'independent reading' section of these notes. Ask children to tell you ways that they might work out the words. Did they suggest breaking the words up into syllables? Did they split the words up into phonemes?

Assessment *(R, AF1)* Do children pronounce 'talents' correctly?

Objective Use syntax and context to build their store of vocabulary when reading for meaning (7.4).

You will need the following words written on word cards: 'character', 'appeal', 'invented', 'illustrated', 'published', 'invaders'.

- **C** *(Clarifying)* Ask the children to scan the text to find one of the words and try to deduce the meaning from the context.

- Ask: *Where can we look to find out what a word means?*

- Ask the children to write down their definition of the word and to check it in a dictionary. Remind them to also check against the 'glossary bubbles' in the book.

Assessment *(R, AF1)* Can they work out what the word means by its context?

Objectives *(Imagining)* Engage with books through exploring and enacting interpretations (8.2).

- **C** Look at pages 6 and pages 10 and 11. Talk about how Mary Tourtel and Charles Schulz gradually added more and more characters to their comic strip as they invented more and more stories.

- Ask the children to either invent a new friend for Rupert Bear or for Charlie Brown. They must think about the character's name, what they look like and what sort of character they are, e.g. quiet and shy or loud and confident.

- Encourage them to draw the character and add labels to describe their character.

Assessment *(R, AF3)* Do children use the text to work out suitable Peanuts or Rupert Bear characters?

Speaking and listening activities

Objective Speak with clarity and use appropriate intonation when reading and reciting texts (1.1).

You will need some comic strips from children's comics that would be suitable for children to act out.

- Give out short sections of a comic strip story to small groups of children. Make sure there is a part for every child in the group to act out.

- Encourage groups to read and act out the comic strip they have been allocated.

- Check that they think about the voice and character of the comic strip character they are acting out.

Cross-curricular links: National Curriculum Key Stage 1

Art and Design
Pupils should be taught to:

- Try out tools and techniques and apply these to materials and processes including drawing

Writing activities

Objectives Use planning to establish clear sections for writing (10.1).
Use appropriate language to make sections hang together (10.2).

You will need an A4 piece of paper divided into six sections with the following words in each section, as shown:

1. First	2. Then	3. Next
4. So	5. After that	6. In the end

- Explain that the children are going to write a short Rupert Bear comic strip adventure.

- Remind the children of the types of adventures that Rupert has, e.g. fairy tales.

- Show the A4 piece of paper and talk about how the comic strip layout is a good way of planning a story. Talk about each of the words in the sections and how this helps structure the story.

- Encourage the children to plan their story and retell it in a comic strip format using speech bubbles.

Assessment *(W, AF3)* Do the children's stories have a beginning, middle and end?

Training Like an Athlete

> **C** = Language comprehension   *R, AF* = QCA reading assessment focus
>
> **W** = Word recognition   *W, AF* = QCA writing assessment focus

Group or guided reading

Introducing the book

C *(Clarifying)* Look at the cover and read the title together. Ask: *What sport is this person playing? Is she an athlete? What is an athlete?*

C *(Prediction)* Ask: *What do you think this book is going to be about?*

Strategy check

Remind the children to break up words into syllables to read new words.

Independent reading

● Ask children to read the book aloud. Praise and encourage them while they read, and prompt as necessary.

C *(Summarising)* Ask them to take note of the ways that the sports people train.

W Remind the children that the bold words are glossary words and that they can look up their meaning at the back of the book.

Assessment Check that the children:

● *(R, AF1)* read high frequency words with confidence

● *(R, AF1)* use a variety of strategies to work out new words

● *(R, AF2)* use comprehension skills to retrieve information.

Returning to the text

C *(Summarising)* Ask: *Was the information in the book as you predicted?* Discuss children's predictions and how close they were to the content of the book. Were there things they expected which weren't in the book?

(C) *(Clarifying, Imagining, Questioning)* Ask children to tell you some different ways that the sports people train. Ask: *What sort of training would you like best? Do you think it is easy to be a top sports person?*

(W) On page 5 ask the children to find the word 'practise'. On page 20 ask them to find the word 'practice' in the heading. Talk about the differences between the words – how the first is a verb (a doing word) and the second is a noun (a thing).

(C) *(Clarifying)* Other than keeping fit ask the children what else sports people need to do. Encourage them to find out by rereading page 21. Ask: *What does it mean 'healthy foods'? Give me an example of a healthy food.*

Group and independent reading activities

Objective Draw together ideas and information from across a whole text, using simple signposts in the text (7.1).

(C) *(Clarifying)* In pairs, ask the children to select two of the four sports people in the book. They must then make comparisons between the two by placing information under headings. The headings could be 'motto', 'hero', 'training', 'when started', 'competitiveness'.

- Encourage and remind children to use the Contents and Index to find information.

- Discuss the information they manage to sort.

- Ask: *In what ways are these sports people similar? In what ways are they different? What do you most admire about these sports people?*

Assessment *(R, AF2)* Do children use the Contents and Index to find the answers to the questions?

(W) Spell with increasing accuracy and confidence, drawing on word recognition and knowledge of word structure, and spelling patterns including use of double letters (6.1).

- Turn to page 13 and ask the children to find you some words on the page where the letters have been doubled when a suffix has been added. They should find 'really' and 'hitting'.

- Ask children to tell you the root word and to explain what has happened when the suffix has been added in each case.
- Ask them to tell you other words that follow the same pattern.
- Look at the word 'interrupt' from the same page. Ask: *Is the 'r' doubled for the same reason?* (no) *Can you explain why not?*

Assessment *(R, AF1)* Do children select/find other relevant examples of doubling letters?

Objective Explain organisational features of texts, including diagrams (7.3).

- **C** *(Clarifying)* Turn to page 7 and reread the series of instructions.
- Ask: *Do you find the photograph to go with each instruction helpful? Is this what you do when you kick a ball? Is there anything else that could be added to the instructions which would help?*
- Look at page 15 and compare these instructions with the ones on page 7. Ask: *What makes these instructions a bit harder to understand?* (6 written instructions and only 3 photos) *What has been added to the photographs which is not on the photographs on page 7?* (numbers)
- Ask the children whether they have any alternative ideas for how the football top tips could be laid out, e.g. just the photographs with labels, just the text, just one drawing with the whole movement of the leg showing, etc.
- Encourage children to plan out their own 'football training tip' instructions.

Assessment *(R, AF2)* Can a partner follow the instructions described?

Objective Explain their reactions to texts, commenting on important aspects (8.3).

- **C** *(Summarising, Imagining)* Ask: *What do all these sports people have which has helped them to succeed?*
- Discuss how the sports people all have determination – that they keep trying and practising until they have got it right.
- Ask: *How do you feel after reading this book? Have you learned something? Is it good to keep trying and trying again at something?*

- Ask the children to think of a realistic target they can work towards through practice and determination. They must write down their target, the date they started and the date they achieved the target.

Assessment (R, AF3) Do children take information from the book and translate it to make it relevant to their lives?

Speaking and listening activities

Objective Listen to others in class, ask relevant questions (2.1).
Adopt appropriate roles in small or large groups (4.1).

- Invite four children to sit in the hot seat as each of the sports people mentioned in the book.
- Encourage the other children to ask the sports people questions based on the information they have learned from the book.

Cross-curricular links: National Curriculum Key Stage 1

PE
Pupils should be taught:

- How important it is to be active

Writing activities

Objective Select from different presentational features to suit particular writing purposes on paper and on screen (9.5).

- Some of the sports people in the book have a motto. David Beckham's is 'Practise, practise, practise'; Ian Thorpe's is 'What you put in is what you get out'.
- Discuss what a motto is and ask the children to think up a motto for themselves. Remind them that it needs to be something that sounds good, is easy to remember and is relevant to them.
- Encourage them to write their motto using a word processing program or neatly on an A4 piece of paper. They can decorate it and make it look eye-catching too.

Assessment (W, AF7) Do children make sensible and effective word choices?

Environmental Disasters

Group or guided reading

Introducing the book

C *(Clarifying)* Look at the cover and read the title together. Ask: *What does disaster mean? Give me an example of a disaster. What do you think environmental means? How does the photograph of the duck on the cover and the fish on the title page help you work out what environmental means?*

C *(Prediction)* Ask: *What do you think has caused the duck to look like this and the fish to have died?*

Strategy check

Remind children of the main ways of finding information in a non-fiction book: by looking in the Contents and Index.

Independent reading

● Ask children to read the book aloud. Praise and encourage them while they read, and prompt as necessary.

C *(Summarising)* Ask them to note whether it was always possible to clear up each of the disasters after they happened.

W Remind children that the bold words are glossary words and that they can look up their meaning at the back of the book.

W Help children with the tricky words 'Exxon Valdez', 'toxic', 'Bhopal', 'Chernobyl' and 'bronchitis'.

Assessment Check that children:

● *(R, AF1)* read high frequency words with confidence

● *(R, AF1)* use a variety of strategies to work out new words

● *(R, AF2)* use comprehension skills to retrieve information.

Returning to the text

C *(Summarising, Clarifying)* Ask: *Was it possible to clear up all the disasters? What happened at Bhopal? Are people still becoming ill because of the disaster there?*

C *(Clarifying, Questioning)* Ask: *Why do people need to have oil, nuclear power and chemicals? What wouldn't we be able to do without them?*

W Point out the italicised words on pages 7 and 9. Explain that when the names of ships are printed out they are always in italics.

W Turn to page 13 and ask the children to find the word 'chemicals'. Explain that the 'ch' phoneme makes a 'k' sound. Ask them to think of some other words with the same 'k' sound. (chemistry, chemist.) Look also at 'bronchitis' on page 22 which has the same 'k' sound.

Group and independent reading activities

Objective Draw together ideas and information from across a whole text, using simple signposts in the text (7.1).

C *(Clarifying)* Provide some questions on cards for the children to find the answers to using the Contents and Index, e.g.

Where were helicopters used in the clean-up operation?
Which country is Bhopal in?
In what year was the Great London Smog?
What happens to animals when oil gets onto their fur?
Where did the *Exxon Valdez* hit a reef?

● Encourage the children to think up questions to ask a partner.

Assessment *(R, AF2)* Do children use the Contents and Index to find the answers to the questions?

W Read and spell less common alternative graphemes including trigraphs (5.4), (6.2).

● Ask the children to find another word with three letters making up one sound (page 19 'fire**figh**ters').

● Once they have found this word, can they think of any more words following the same pattern as 'fight'?

Assessment *(R, AF1)* Do children think of 'light', 'night', 'right', etc?

Objective Use syntax and context to build their store of vocabulary when reading for meaning (7.4).

You will need the following words written on word cards: 'fumes', 'toxic', 'radioactive', 'pollution'.

- **C** *(Clarifying)* Ask the children to scan the text to find one of the words and try to deduce the meaning from the context.
- Ask the children to write down their definition of the word and to check it against the glossary in the book and a dictionary.

Assessment *(R, AF1)* Can they work out what the word means by its context?

Objective Engage with books through exploring and enacting interpretations (8.2).

- **C** *(Summarising, Predicting)* Turn to look at the photographs of the animals on pages 5, 8 and 10. Ask: *How do these photographs make you feel?*
- Talk about why seeing these photographs makes people feel very angry that such accidents should happen.

Assessment *(R, AF3)* Children suggest oil spill disasters.

E-links

Fireflies Plus

If you are an Espresso user, you can access videos, quizzes and activities linked to this title to enrich your children's reading. Children can also write, post and compare reviews of the book. Full supporting Teaching Notes for this content are available on the site in PDF format. Within the Espresso site, follow the route **<Channel guide → English 1 → Oxford Reading Tree Fireflies Plus logo>.** *Espresso Primary* is an extensive library of cross-curricular, video-rich broadband teaching resources and learning activities that motivates children and supports teachers.

Speaking and listening activities

Objective Listen to others in class, ask relevant questions (2.1).
Adopt appropriate roles in small or large groups (4.1).

- Invite the children to be TV news reporters reporting on one of the disasters mentioned in the book.

- Encourage them to describe clearly what is happening and to be able to answer questions posed by the children who are listening.

Cross-curricular links: National Curriculum Key Stage 1

Geography
Pupils should be taught to:

- Recognise changes in the environment

Writing activities

Objectives Select from different presentational features to suit particular writing purposes on paper and on screen (9.5).
Write simple and compound sentences (11.1).

You will need some headlines from a quality newspaper.

- Ask the children to choose one of the disasters in the book and write a brief newspaper report about the disaster as an eye witness account.

- Encourage them to use strong descriptive words to describe effectively the enormity of the disaster.

- Remind them to think of an eye-catching headline.

- Show some examples of newspaper headlines to give the children some ideas.

Assessment *(W, AF7)* Do children make sensible and effective word choices?

Oxford Reading Tree resources at this level

Biff, Chip and Kipper
Stage 9 Stories
Stage 9 More Stories A

Poetry
Glow-worms Stage 8–9

Non-fiction
Stage 9 Fireflies
Stage 9 Treetops Non-Fiction

Wider reading
Stage 9 Snapdragons
Stage 9 Treetops Stories
Stage 9a Treetops Stories

Electronic
Stage 8–9 Talking Stories
e-Songbirds
e-Fireflies
MagicPage
Clip Art
ORT Online www.OxfordReadingTree.com

Teachers' Resources
Comprehension Photocopy Masters
(Stages 6–9)
Context Cards
Teacher's Handbook (Stages 1–9)
Group Activity Sheets
Phonics and Spelling Activities (Stages 1–9)
Stage 9 Workbooks
Snapdragons Teaching Notes, Guided
Reading Cards and Parent Notes
Fireflies Teaching Notes

OXFORD
UNIVERSITY PRESS

Great Clarendon Street, Oxford OX2 6DP

Oxford University Press is a department of the University of Oxford. It furthers the University's objective of excellence in research, scholarship, and education by publishing worldwide in

Oxford   New York

Auckland   Cape Town   Dar es Salaam   Hong Kong   Karachi
Kuala Lumpur   Madrid   Melbourne   Mexico City   Nairobi
New Delhi   Shanghai   Taipei   Toronto

With offices in

Argentina   Austria   Brazil   Chile   Czech Republic   France
Greece   Guatemala   Hungary   Italy   Japan   Poland
Portugal   Singapore   South Korea   Switzerland
Thailand   Turkey   Ukraine   Vietnam

Oxford is a registered trade mark of Oxford University Press in the UK and in certain other countries

Text © Oxford University Press 2008

Written by Lucy Tritton

The moral rights of the author have been asserted

Database right Oxford University Press (maker)

First published 2008

British Library Cataloguing in Publication Data

Data available

ISBN 978-0-19-847332-9

10 9 8 7 6 5 4 3 2

Page make-up by Thomson Digital

Printed in China

Paper used in the production of this book is a natural, recyclable product made from wood grown in sustainable forests. The manufacturing process conforms to the environmental regulations of the country of origin.